Table of Contents

Module 9: Financial Recovery

Module 10: Relapse Prevention

Module 11: Building a New Life

Appendices

Introduction

Welcome · How to Use This Workbook · Note on Cultural Responsiveness

Welcome Letter

Dear Friend,

Thank you for picking up this workbook. I know that doing so may not have been easy. Whether you were handed this by a counselor, found it on your own, or were encouraged by someone who cares about you, the fact that you are here — holding these pages — is an act of courage. Please do not underestimate that.

My name is James Martinez. I am a licensed counselor who has spent many years working alongside individuals and families navigating the very real and very painful challenges of gambling addiction. I have seen the shame, the secrecy, the financial devastation, the fractured relationships, and the quiet despair that so often accompany this disorder. I have also witnessed — time and again — something more powerful than all of that: the extraordinary resilience of human beings who decide that things can be different.

This workbook was developed using evidence-based clinical approaches, including Cognitive Behavioral Therapy (CBT), Motivational Interviewing (MI), and Solution-Focused Therapy. Each of these frameworks has a strong research base demonstrating effectiveness in the treatment of gambling disorder. The modules ahead draw from the best of what the clinical literature has to offer, translated into accessible, practical tools that you can use in your daily life.

You do not have to be "ready" in the way you might imagine. Recovery is not a single moment of dramatic transformation. It is a series of small decisions, made day after day, that gradually create a new way of living. All you need to begin is the willingness to try — and that willingness is something you already have, simply by opening this page.

I also want you to know that this workbook was designed with you specifically in mind — not a generic "person with a gambling problem," but a real, complex human being with your own history, culture, values, relationships, and strengths. The exercises and reflections here are invitations, not requirements. You are encouraged to bring your whole self to this work.

Your journey toward healing begins here. Take it one page, one day, one moment at a time.

With hope and respect,

James Martinez, MS, LCADC, LSATP, CAADC, CASAC-II, ICGC

How to Use This Workbook

This workbook is designed to be a flexible, comprehensive companion for your recovery journey. It can be used in one of two ways:

1. **With a counselor or therapist:** Each module can serve as the basis for individual counseling sessions, group therapy, or psychoeducational programming. Your counselor may assign specific modules, worksheets, or exercises between sessions to reinforce the work done in the clinical setting.
2. **Independently:** If you are working through this workbook on your own, that is entirely appropriate. You may proceed at whatever pace feels manageable. Some modules may take one sitting; others may require several days of reflection. There is no timeline — only your timeline.

A few important guidelines:

- Each module builds on the one before it. While you may be drawn to skip ahead, it is recommended that you work through the modules in order, particularly the early modules on self-assessment, honesty, and triggers.
- Honesty is the single most essential ingredient in this process. The worksheets and reflection exercises are only as valuable as the honesty you bring to them. There are no right or wrong answers — only your truth.
- This workbook is a tool, not a test. You will not be graded. You cannot fail. Every honest response you write, no matter how difficult or incomplete, is a step forward.
- If a question or exercise brings up strong emotions, that is normal and even expected. Give yourself permission to pause, breathe, and return when you are ready. If you are working with a counselor, bring those difficult moments to your sessions.

- Keep this workbook private and in a safe place. Your responses are deeply personal and deserve to be protected.

Note on Cultural Responsiveness

Gambling addiction does not discriminate. It affects individuals across every culture, ethnicity, socioeconomic background, age group, gender identity, spiritual tradition, and life circumstance. The experience of gambling disorder — and the path to recovery — is shaped in important ways by the cultural context in which a person lives. What gambling means in one community may be very different from what it means in another. Family dynamics, community attitudes toward help-seeking, spiritual beliefs, and cultural values around money, luck, and success all influence how gambling disorder develops and how recovery unfolds.

This workbook has been designed to respect and affirm that diversity. The exercises and reflections here are intentionally open-ended, allowing you to bring your own cultural framework, spiritual beliefs, and personal values to the work. If a particular exercise does not resonate with your cultural background, you are encouraged to adapt it in a way that does. There is no single "correct" path to recovery — there is only the path that is authentic and meaningful for you.

If your cultural background, religious tradition, or family values play a significant role in your relationship with gambling, consider how they might also be a source of strength and support in your recovery.

Module 1: Understanding Gambling Addiction

What Is Gambling Addiction · The Gambling Chain · My Gambling History · Cultural Myths About Gambling

1.1 What Is Gambling Addiction?

Gambling disorder is a recognized behavioral addiction classified in the Diagnostic and Statistical Manual of Mental Disorders, Fifth Edition (DSM-5) by the American Psychiatric Association. It is the only behavioral addiction formally classified alongside substance use disorders — a designation that reflects the growing body of neurobiological evidence demonstrating that gambling disorder shares key features with substance addiction, including effects on the brain's reward circuitry, patterns of escalation and withdrawal, and profound impacts on functioning and quality of life.

At the neurological level, gambling activates the brain's dopamine reward system in ways that are strikingly similar to psychoactive drugs. The anticipation of a win triggers a surge of dopamine — the neurotransmitter associated with pleasure and motivation. Over time, the brain adapts to these surges by requiring larger and larger stimulation to achieve the same effect, a phenomenon known as tolerance. When the person is not gambling, they may experience restlessness, irritability, and a sense of emotional flatness — a withdrawal-like state that drives them back to gambling for relief.

The addiction cycle typically unfolds as follows: **Excitement** (the thrill of placing a bet) → **Loss** (losing money, which intensifies the urge to win it back) → **Chasing** (continuing to gamble in pursuit of recovery) → **Shame** (guilt, self-loathing, and concealment) → **Return to Gambling** (using gambling to escape the shame). This cycle becomes self-perpetuating and increasingly difficult to interrupt without clinical intervention.

To meet the DSM-5 criteria for gambling disorder, an individual must exhibit four or more of the following within a 12-month period:

- Needing to gamble with increasing amounts of money in order to achieve the desired excitement.
- Being restless or irritable when attempting to cut down or stop gambling.
- Making repeated unsuccessful efforts to control, cut back, or stop gambling.
- Being preoccupied with gambling (e.g., reliving past gambling experiences, planning the next gambling venture, thinking about ways to get money with which to gamble).
- Often gambling when feeling distressed (e.g., feelings of helplessness, guilt, anxiety, or depression).
- After losing money gambling, often returning another day to get even ("chasing" one's losses).
- Lying to conceal the extent of involvement with gambling.
- Jeopardizing or losing a significant relationship, job, or educational or career opportunity because of gambling.
- Relying on others to provide money to relieve desperate financial situations caused by gambling.

Clinical Note **Gambling disorder exists on a spectrum of severity: Mild (4–5 criteria), Moderate (6–7 criteria), and Severe (8–9 criteria). Regardless of where on the spectrum a person falls, the disorder is real, serious, and — critically — treatable. Recovery is possible at every stage.**

1.2 The Gambling Chain

The Gambling Chain is a cognitive-behavioral model that maps the sequence of events leading from a trigger to the consequences of gambling — and back again. Understanding this chain is foundational to recovery, because breaking any single link in the chain can interrupt the entire addiction cycle.

TRIGGER		THOUGHT		URGE
Person, place, emotion, or situation that activates the urge	→	"I need to gamble. I deserve it. Just this once."	→	Intense craving; physical and emotional pressure to gamble
RETURN TO GAMBLING		SHAME		CONSEQUENCE
Shame fuels the next round of escape through gambling	←	Guilt, self-loathing, concealment; the emotional aftermath	←	Financial loss, relationship damage, broken promises

Below the table, one additional link connects back upward:

BEHAVIOR
The act of gambling itself: placing the bet, entering the casino, going online

Explaining Each Link:

- **Trigger:** The starting point — any internal state (stress, boredom, loneliness) or external cue (a casino advertisement, payday, driving past a betting shop) that initiates the chain. Triggers are highly personal and vary widely between individuals.
- **Thought:** The automatic thoughts and cognitive distortions (rationalizations, justifications) that follow the trigger and make gambling seem reasonable or necessary in the moment. These thoughts are often rapid, habitual, and largely unconscious.
- **Urge:** The intense craving that follows. Urges are time-limited — they peak and subside, typically within 15–30 minutes — but they feel permanent and overwhelming in the moment.

- **Behavior:** The act of gambling itself. At this point, the individual has moved from internal experience to external action.
- **Consequence:** The real-world results of gambling — financial loss, broken commitments, damaged relationships, and the worsening of the very problems gambling was meant to solve.
- **Shame:** The emotional aftermath: guilt, humiliation, self-criticism, and secrecy. Shame is one of the most powerful drivers of continued gambling, because gambling provides temporary relief from the very shame it creates.
- **Return to Gambling:** Shame fuels the next round. The cycle continues — and typically escalates.

Recovery Key: Breaking the Chain

Recovery does not require that you eliminate every trigger — that is impossible. It requires learning to *break the chain* at any point. You can challenge the thought before it becomes an urge. You can ride out the urge using coping skills before it becomes a behavior. You can interrupt a behavior before the full consequences unfold. Every link is a point of intervention. Every module in this workbook provides tools to break the chain at a different point.

1.3 Worksheet: My Gambling History

✎ Worksheet 1.3 — My Gambling History

Take your time with this worksheet. There are no right or wrong answers. Be as honest as you can. Your responses are for your benefit alone.

When did you first gamble?

How old were you?

What was the situation?

____

What types of gambling have you engaged in? (check all that apply)

☐ Slot Machines ☐ Table Games (blackjack, roulette, etc.) ☐ Sports Betting

☐ Lottery / Scratch Tickets ☐ Online Gambling / Casino Apps ☐ Poker

☐ Horse / Dog Racing ☐ Bingo ☐ Other:

When did gambling start to feel like a problem?

What is the most you have lost in a single day? $

What is the most you have lost in a single month? $

How has gambling affected your finances?

____

How has gambling affected your relationships?

____

How has gambling affected your work or daily responsibilities?

____

What do you hope to accomplish by completing this workbook?

____

1.4 Reflection Exercise: Cultural Myths About Gambling

Many people hold beliefs about gambling that are shaped by culture, media, family, and personal experience. These beliefs — myths — can make it harder to recognize gambling as a problem and harder to seek help. Review each myth below and the clinical reframe that

Myth	Clinical Reframe
"Gambling is just	The DSM-5 recognizes gambling disorder as a diagnosable behavioral

entertainment — it's not a real addiction."	addiction with neurobiological underpinnings identical to substance use disorders. For millions of people, gambling is far beyond entertainment — it is a compulsive behavior that causes serious harm.
"I can beat the system if I'm smart enough."	All gambling games are mathematically engineered to favor the house. No strategy, intelligence, or system can overcome a built-in statistical edge over the long term. The belief that skill alone can beat the house is called the "illusion of control" — a well-documented cognitive distortion.
"Winners are just lucky — and I could be lucky too."	Casino environments are carefully designed to make winners visible and losers invisible. For every jackpot winner, tens of thousands of people lose significant money that day. Selective attention to wins creates a distorted picture of gambling reality.
"It's not as serious as drug or alcohol addiction."	Gambling disorder carries among the highest suicide rates of any psychiatric condition — studies suggest 20% or more of those with gambling disorder attempt suicide. Financial devastation, family destruction, and mental health crisis are common. The severity is comparable to severe substance use disorders.
"I can stop whenever I want — I just choose not to."	This is one of the defining features of addiction: the subjective sense of control, combined with the objective inability to stop despite negative consequences. The belief that one can "choose" to stop at any time is a

hallmark of denial, not evidence of control.

"Gambling is part of my culture — there's nothing wrong with it."	Cultural and social norms around gambling vary widely, and recreational gambling is not inherently harmful for everyone. However, when gambling causes harm — financial, relational, psychological — it has crossed from cultural practice into addiction, regardless of cultural context.
"Real gamblers are old men in smoky casinos — that's not me."	Gambling disorder affects people across all ages, genders, ethnicities, and socioeconomic backgrounds. It is increasingly prevalent among young adults due to the rise of online gambling and sports betting apps. There is no single profile of a "problem gambler."
"If I could just get one big win, I could pay everything back and stop."	This is "chasing" — one of the core behavioral markers of gambling disorder. Research consistently shows that even when gamblers win significant sums, they typically continue gambling until the money is gone. The problem is not the debt — it is the compulsion.

✎ Reflection: Cultural Myths About Gambling

Which of these myths have you believed?

Which resonated most with your own thinking?

How has that belief affected you — your gambling behavior, your ability to seek help, or your understanding of your situation?

Module 2: Self-Assessment and Acceptance

Personal Assessment · Consequences · Balance of Change · Readiness for Change

2.1 Personal Assessment

The following self-assessment is adapted from validated clinical screening tools used in the assessment of gambling disorder. Read each question carefully and respond honestly. This is not a diagnostic instrument — it is a tool for self-reflection. Your responses are for your benefit.

#	Question	Yes	No
1	Have you ever felt the need to bet more and more money to get the same feeling of excitement?		
2	Have you ever gone back another day to try to win back money you lost?		
3	Have you ever borrowed money or sold something to finance gambling?		
4	Have you ever felt you might have a problem with gambling?		
5	Has gambling ever caused you to have health problems, including stress or anxiety?		
6	Have people ever criticized your betting or told you that you had a gambling problem, whether or not you thought it was true?		
7	Has your gambling ever caused financial problems for you or your household?		
8	Have you ever felt guilty about the way you gamble or what happens when you gamble?		

9	Has gambling ever caused you to lose time from work, school, or family commitments?
10	Have you ever hidden gambling activities or money from family members or others important in your life?

Score	Interpretation
0–2 Yes	Low level of problem. Monitoring and preventive education recommended.
3–4 Yes	Moderate concern. Some problem gambling behaviors are present. Consider speaking with a counselor.
5–7 Yes	Problem gambling is likely. Professional assessment and support are strongly recommended.
8–10 Yes	Significant gambling disorder indicators. Professional clinical intervention is recommended as soon as possible.

My score: ______ My reaction to this score:

2.2 Consequences of Gambling in My Life

Gambling disorder touches every area of a person's life. Use the table below to reflect on how gambling has affected each domain. Be as specific and honest as you can.

Area of Life	How Gambling Has Affected Me
Financial	-
Relationships	

Work or Career

Physical Health

Mental Health

Legal

Spiritual

Looking at this table, what surprises you most? Which area of consequences feels most urgent to address?

2.3 The Balance of Change

One of the most honest things you can do in early recovery is to acknowledge that gambling has provided something — excitement, escape, hope, or relief — even as it has caused tremendous harm. The decisional balance exercise below invites you to explore both sides with complete honesty. There are no wrong answers. Filling this in honestly is itself a courageous act.

	Benefits / Pros	**Costs / Cons**
Continuing to Gamble		
Stopping Gambling		

After completing this exercise, what stands out to you?

2.4 My Readiness for Change Scale

The Transtheoretical Model of Change describes the stages through which people typically move when modifying a behavior. Understanding where you are in this process — without judgment — is an important step toward moving forward.

Precontemplation

"I don't believe I have a gambling problem."

Not yet seeing the problem, minimizing consequences, may feel defensive or resistant. May be in this workbook at someone else's urging.

Contemplation

"I'm thinking that gambling might be a problem, but I'm not sure I want to change."

Awareness is growing, but ambivalence is strong. Weighing the pros and cons. May feel stuck or conflicted.

Preparation

"I know I need to change and I'm getting ready to take steps."

Beginning to plan for change. May be reducing gambling, researching help options, or telling someone about the problem.

Action

"I am actively working to stop gambling and change my life."

In treatment, attending Gamblers Anonymous, using coping skills, making direct changes in behavior and environment.

Maintenance

"I have stopped gambling and I am working to sustain my recovery."

Continued vigilance against relapse, building a new lifestyle, deepening coping skills and support systems.

✎ My Readiness for Change

Which stage am I in right now?____

My readiness for change on a scale of 1–10 (1 = not ready at all, 10 = fully committed):

Reflection Questions for My Current Stage:

If Precontemplation: What would need to happen for me to consider that gambling might be a problem?____

____

If Contemplation: What are the top three reasons I might want to change? What holds me back?____

____

If Preparation: What specific steps do I need to take this week to move toward action?____

____

If Action: What am I doing that is working? What support do I still need?__________

____

If Maintenance: What are my biggest ongoing risks? How do I stay vigilant?_________

____

Module 3: Honesty as a Core Recovery Skill

The Role of Honesty · Self-Deception · Honesty Assessment · Denial · Radical Honesty · Accountability

3.1 The Role of Honesty in Recovery

Honesty is not just a virtue — it is a foundational clinical skill in addiction recovery. Without honesty, recovery cannot take root. Addiction does not merely cause dishonesty; it depends on it. The gambling addiction cycle is sustained by a carefully constructed architecture of deception that operates on three levels:

Level 1: Dishonesty with Self (Self-Deception)

Self-deception is the foundation of addictive behavior. It includes minimizing ("It's not that bad"), rationalizing ("I deserve this"), denying ("I can stop whenever I want"), and distorting reality ("The next win will fix everything"). Self-deception allows the individual to continue gambling while maintaining a fragile self-image.

Level 2: Dishonesty with Others

As gambling escalates, lies to loved ones become necessary to protect the addiction. These lies range from small omissions ("I didn't mention where I was") to elaborate fabrications ("The money went to car repairs"). Each lie creates distance in relationships and deepens isolation.

Level 3: Dishonesty in Recovery

Perhaps the most dangerous form: lying to therapists, counselors, sponsors, or group members. This includes minimizing gambling activity during treatment, presenting a false image of progress, or withholding critical information. Dishonesty in recovery renders treatment ineffective.

The "Wall of Lies"

Over time, the accumulation of lies creates what clinicians call a "wall of lies" — a barrier between the addicted individual and genuine connection with others. This wall serves two purposes: it protects the addiction, and it protects the individual from the pain of facing the truth. But this protection comes at an enormous cost. Behind the wall, isolation deepens, shame intensifies, and the addiction grows stronger.

Recovery requires dismantling this wall — brick by brick, lie by lie. This is painful work. But it is essential work. Every truth told, no matter how small, loosens a brick. Every honest conversation is an act of recovery.

3.2 The Self-Deception Inventory

Check every statement below that has applied to you, honestly and without judgment. This inventory is for your eyes only.

☐	**Self-Deception Statement**
☐	I can stop gambling whenever I want to — I just don't want to right now.
☐	I'm only gambling for entertainment; it's not a real problem.
☐	I'll win it all back next time. I just had bad luck today.

☐ My gambling doesn't hurt anyone but me.

☐ I deserve to have some fun after everything I've been through.

☐ Gambling is the only thing that relieves my stress.

☐ I'm not as bad as other gamblers I've seen.

☐ I have a system — I just need to refine it.

☐ Once I pay off this debt, I'll quit for good.

☐ I'm just going through a rough patch; it'll get better on its own.

☐ I only gamble what I can afford to lose.

☐ My family doesn't understand — they're overreacting.

☐ If I had more money, gambling wouldn't be a problem.

☐ I'm smarter than the average gambler — I know what I'm doing.

☐ Things will be different this time.

Checked Items	Interpretation
0–3	Low level of self-deception currently present, or high level of self-awareness. Continue building honesty skills.
4–7	Moderate self-deception. Several protective beliefs are maintaining the addiction cycle. This module's exercises will be particularly valuable.
8–11	Significant self-deception is present. The architecture of denial is strong. Working closely with a counselor and/or sponsor is recommended.
12–15	High self-deception. Denial is operating powerfully. Consider that the very

act of checking this many items honestly may be an important beginning.

3.3 Worksheet: My Honesty Assessment

✎ Worksheet 3.3 — My Honesty Assessment

In what areas of my life have I been dishonest because of gambling?_______________

____

Who have I lied to because of gambling?_______________________________

What have those lies been about?_______________________________

What have I hidden — from others and from myself?_____________________

____

What truth have I been avoiding about myself and my gambling?_______________

____

How has dishonesty protected my addiction?______________________________

____

What would it mean — in practical, daily terms — to be fully honest?__________

____

3.4 Breaking Through Denial

Denial is not a character flaw — it is a psychological defense mechanism. The brain naturally protects us from information that is too painful to integrate all at once. In gambling disorder, denial operates to shield the person from the full weight of consequences, allowing the addiction to continue. Breaking through denial is not about shame or confrontation — it is a gradual process of allowing truth to enter, one piece at a time.

Stages of Denial in Gambling Addiction:

1. **Total Denial:** "I don't have a problem."
2. **Minimizing:** "It's not that bad — other people have it worse."
3. **Rationalizing:** "I have good reasons for gambling."
4. **Blaming:** "My gambling is caused by stress / my relationship / my job."

5. **Bargaining:** "I'll cut back — I just won't quit entirely."
6. **Acceptance:** "I have a problem, and I need help."

Denial Statement	Clinical Reframe
"I only gamble what I can afford."	If gambling were affordable, the financial consequences described elsewhere in this workbook would not exist. The addiction distorts our accounting of what we "can afford."
"I've never gambled at work or during work hours."	Addiction does not require 24/7 engagement to be serious. Its impact is measured by harm, not by frequency or timing.
"My family is exaggerating."	Those closest to us often see the impact of our behavior before we do. Their concern is data worth considering, not bias to be dismissed.
"I stopped for three months — so I'm not addicted."	The ability to stop temporarily is not evidence of the absence of addiction. What matters is the pattern over time and the compulsive return to gambling.

✎ Reflection: Denial

Which stage of denial most closely describes where you have been? Where are you now?____

____

What truth about your gambling are you most resistant to acknowledging?

____

3.5 Practicing Radical Honesty

Radical honesty — in the context of addiction recovery — means committing to a practice of telling the truth about your gambling, your emotions, your thoughts, and your actions, even when it is uncomfortable. It is not about brutal candor for its own sake; it is about eliminating the deception that sustains addiction and replacing it with authentic connection.

Five Daily Exercises for Building Honesty:

1. **The Honesty Journal:** Each evening, write one thing that was true about your day — something you might have been tempted to hide or minimize. It need not be dramatic. The habit of honest daily reflection is transformative over time.
2. **Making Amends for a Small Lie:** Choose one minor dishonesty from the past week — something small that you can acknowledge without catastrophizing. Correct it. Notice how it feels.
3. **Sharing a Difficult Truth:** Identify one honest thing — about your feelings, your struggles, or your day — and share it with a trusted person. Not to confess, but to connect.
4. **The Pause Practice:** Before speaking in a situation where you might be tempted to minimize or deceive, pause for three breaths. Ask yourself: "Is what I'm about to say true?" Practice saying the true thing, even imperfectly.
5. **The End-of-Day Honesty Check:** Ask yourself these three questions each night: "Did I tell the truth today? Did I act in alignment with my recovery? Is there anything I need to correct or acknowledge?"

3.6 Building Accountability Structures

Recovery cannot be sustained in isolation. Accountability structures — relationships and commitments that create external support for honest behavior — are a critical component of long-term recovery. Research consistently shows that individuals with strong accountability supports achieve better outcomes.

Accountability structures may include: an accountability partner (a trusted friend or family member), a sponsor (from Gamblers Anonymous or a similar program), a therapist or counselor, or a group therapy setting. The key element is consistent, honest reporting of your recovery status to someone who cares about your wellbeing.

✎ My Accountability Plan

My accountability partner (name): ______________________ Contact number:_______________ We will

check in: ☐ Daily ☐ Every few days ☐ Weekly During our check-ins, I commit to being honest

about: ______________________ If I have a slip or am struggling, I will contact this person within: ____

hours. My commitment to this accountability relationship: ______________________

Module 4: Identifying My Triggers

Types of Triggers · Trigger Log · Personal Trigger Map · Stimulus Control

4.1 Types of Triggers

A trigger is any cue — internal or external — that activates the urge to gamble. Understanding your personal triggers is one of the most practical steps you can take in early recovery. You cannot avoid what you cannot name. Triggers are not causes of gambling in themselves — but they are the starting point of the gambling chain, and recognizing them gives you a powerful point of intervention.

Internal Triggers	External Triggers
Emotional States: Anxiety, depression, loneliness, boredom, excitement, anger, grief, guilt, hopelessness, elation **Thought Patterns:** "Just once won't hurt," "I deserve this," "I need to win back what I lost," gambling fantasies, memories of big wins	**People:** Gambling companions, family members who enable, anyone who has gambled with you **Places:** Casinos, racetracks, lottery retailers, sports bars, online betting sites, ATMs near gambling venues **Times & Events:** Paydays, weekends, tax refunds, sporting events,

Physical States:

Fatigue, pain, hunger, alcohol/substance use, insomnia, physical tension

anniversaries, holidays, "free time"

Situations:

Financial stress, arguments with family, work pressure, periods of success or good fortune

4.2 Trigger Log Worksheet

Use this log for one week to track situations in which you experience gambling urges. The goal is awareness, not perfection. You do not need to have gambled to complete an entry — in fact, the most valuable entries are when you experienced an urge and did NOT gamble.

Date	Time	Situation / Where I Was	Internal State (Emotions / Thoughts)	Urge Intensity (1-10)	What I Did?	What Helped?

4.3 Map of My Personal Triggers

✎ **Worksheet 4.3 — My Personal Trigger Map**

In each category below, identify the specific triggers that apply to YOU. Be as concrete and specific as possible.

Emotional Triggers (Which feelings drive you to gamble?)

Social Triggers (Which people or social situations trigger urges?)

Environmental Triggers (Which places, sounds, or sights trigger urges?)

Financial Triggers (Which financial situations trigger urges?)

Time-Based Triggers (Which times of day, week, or year are highest risk?) Anniversary / Event

Triggers (Specific dates, events, or seasons?)

My single highest-risk trigger is:

My plan for managing that trigger:

4.4 Stimulus Control Exercise

Stimulus control is a behavioral strategy that involves reducing your exposure to gambling-related cues and restructuring your environment to support recovery. The core principle is simple: if you are not around gambling cues, urges are less likely to be triggered. Stimulus control is not a permanent state of avoidance — it is a strategic restructuring of your environment during the vulnerable early stages of recovery.

Complete the table below for your five most significant triggers:

Trigger	Avoidability (1=very hard, 5=very easy)	Specific Avoidance or Management Plan
1. ______________		
2. ______________		

3.

____

4.

____

5.

____

Module 5: Cognitive Restructuring

Thinking and Gambling · Thought Record · Challenging Gambling Thoughts · The Math of Gambling

5.1 Thinking and Gambling

At the heart of gambling disorder is a pattern of distorted thinking — automatic thoughts and beliefs that make gambling seem rational, necessary, or inevitable when it is none of these things. Cognitive Behavioral Therapy (CBT) is among the most well-researched and effective approaches to gambling disorder, and its central mechanism is the identification and restructuring of these distorted thought patterns.

Common Cognitive Distortions in Gambling:

- **The Gambler's Fallacy:** The belief that past events influence future random outcomes. ("I've lost ten times in a row — I'm due for a win.") In reality, each spin, roll, or hand is an independent event with identical odds.
- **Illusion of Control:** The belief that personal skill, knowledge, rituals, or strategies can influence inherently random outcomes. ("I have a system." "I can feel when the machine is about to hit.") This is one of the most powerful drivers of continued gambling.
- **Selective Memory for Wins:** The tendency to vividly remember wins and minimize or forget losses. This creates a distorted internal ledger that overestimates past success and feeds the expectation of future wins.
- **Superstitious Thinking:** Beliefs that specific behaviors, clothing, seats, or rituals influence gambling outcomes. These beliefs are reinforced by random coincidences ("I won when I wore this shirt") and persist despite contrary evidence.
- **Chasing:** The belief that continued gambling is the rational response to losses — "I need to win back what I lost." In reality, each subsequent bet is an independent new loss risk, and chasing dramatically increases total losses.

5.2 Thought Record Worksheet

Use this CBT thought record to identify and challenge gambling-related automatic thoughts. A worked example is provided in the first row.

Situation	Automatic Thought	Emotion & Intensity (%)	Cognitive Distortion Type	Balanced Alternative Thought	Outcome / How I Feel Now
Received paycheck. Drove past the casino on the way home.	*"I've worked hard this week — I deserve to treat myself. Just an hour."*	*Excitement 75%, Guilt 40%*	*Rationalization / Entitlement Thinking*	*"Gambling is not a reward — it's a risk I can't afford. My real reward is keeping this money and paying my bills."*	*Anxiety reduced to 30%. I drove home a different route.*

5.3 Challenging My Gambling Thoughts

Below are ten of the most common gambling-related cognitive distortions. For each one, read the statement and then complete the three fill-in fields with your own honest responses. The goal is to develop a personal library of responses to the thoughts that most often precede gambling.

1. "I deserve to gamble — I work hard and I've earned it."

*Why it's a distortion:*____

*A more realistic thought:*____

*How I'll respond next time I have this thought:*____________________________

2. "Just one more bet and I'll stop."

*Why it's a distortion:*____

*A more realistic thought:*____

*How I'll respond:*____

3. "I can win back what I've lost."

*Why it's a distortion:*____

*A more realistic thought:*____

*How I'll respond:*____

4. "Gambling is the only way out of my financial problems."

*Why it's a distortion:*____

*A more realistic thought:*______________________________________

*How I'll respond:*____

5. "I'm a skilled gambler — I have an edge."

*Why it's a distortion:*____

*A more realistic thought:*______________________________________

*How I'll respond:*____

6. "I deserve to have some fun — everyone else does."

*Why it's a distortion:*____

*A more realistic thought:*______________________________________

*How I'll respond:*____

7. "If I quit now, I'll lose all the money I've already put in."

*Why it's a distortion:*____

*A more realistic thought:*____

*How I'll respond:*____

8. "I was so close to winning — I should try again."

*Why it's a distortion:*____

*A more realistic thought:*____

*How I'll respond:*____

9. "It's just entertainment money."

*Why it's a distortion:*____

*A more realistic thought:*____

*How I'll respond:*____

10. "I can control it this time."

*Why it's a distortion:*____

*A more realistic thought:*____

*How I'll respond:*____

5.4 The Math of Gambling

Understanding the mathematics behind gambling can help dismantle the distorted thinking that fuels addiction. The house always has an edge — and over time, this edge guarantees that players lose.

Game	House Edge	What This Means
Slot Machines	2%–15%	For every $100 wagered, the casino keeps $2–$15 on average.
Blackjack (basic strategy)	0.5%–2%	One of the lowest edges — but most players don't use optimal strategy, increasing the effective edge.

Roulette (American, double-zero)	5.26%	The double-zero pocket gives the house its edge on every spin.
Roulette (European, single-zero)	2.70%	Slightly better odds, but the house still wins over time.
Lottery	50%+	Lotteries keep over half of all money wagered. The odds of winning a major jackpot are astronomically small.
Sports Betting	4.5%–10%	The "vig" or "juice" ensures the sportsbook profits regardless of the outcome.
Keno	20%–35%	Among the worst odds in any casino game.
Craps (Pass/Come)	1.41%	Relatively low edge, but side bets can carry edges of 10% or more.

Cost Calculator: What Gambling Really Costs

If you lose an average of $50 per day gambling:

Time Period	Total Lost
1 week	$350
1 month	$1,500
3 months	$4,500
6 months	$9,000
1 year	$18,250
5 years	$91,250
10 years	$182,500

✎ My Personal Cost Calculator

My average daily gambling loss: $__________

My weekly loss: $__________

My monthly loss: $__________

My yearly loss: $__________

Reflection: What would you do with this money if it hadn't been lost to gambling?

____

Module 6: Managing Emotions

Emotions and Gambling · Emotional Thermometer · Regulation Techniques · My Emotional Management Plan

6.1 Emotions and Gambling

One of the most important questions in gambling disorder treatment is: *What function does gambling serve?* For most people struggling with gambling addiction, gambling is not simply about money or excitement — it is a strategy for managing emotions. Gambling is used to escape from painful feelings (boredom, anxiety, depression, loneliness, grief, shame) and sometimes to amplify or sustain positive feelings (excitement, confidence, belonging, euphoria).

This pattern — using gambling to regulate emotional states — is known as emotional avoidance. While it provides temporary relief, emotional avoidance is profoundly counterproductive: it prevents the development of genuine emotion regulation skills, it deepens the underlying emotional problems (since they are never actually addressed), and it creates new painful emotions (shame, guilt, financial anxiety) that in turn drive more gambling.

The goal of this module is to help you build a robust repertoire of genuine emotion regulation skills — so that when difficult emotions arise, you have effective alternatives to gambling.

6.2 Emotional Thermometer

The emotional thermometer is a tool for monitoring your emotional intensity throughout the day. By tracking where you are on the scale — before urges escalate — you can intervene earlier and more effectively. The lower the number, the more resources you have available for coping. The goal is to recognize rising emotional temperature and act before you reach the crisis zone.

Level	Zone	Emotions / Experience	Physical Sensations
10	CRISIS	Out of control, dissociated, in despair, suicidal ideation	Shaking, hyperventilating, chest pain
9	Extreme Distress	Rage, panic, terror, profound shame	Heart pounding, can't think clearly
8	High Distress	Strong urge to gamble, intense anxiety, desperation	Tight chest, stomach knots, sweating
7	Significant Distress	Worry, frustration, shame, loneliness	Muscle tension, restlessness, fatigue
6	Moderate-High	Irritability, low mood, mild urge to gamble	Mild tension, appetite changes
5	Moderate	Boredom, mild anxiety, mild sadness	Slightly tense, low energy
4	Mild Distress	Minor worry, slight restlessness	Mostly comfortable, slightly alert
3	Comfortable	Generally okay, present, engaged	Relaxed, breathing normally
2	Calm	Content, grounded, peaceful	Relaxed body, clear mind
1	Very Calm	Deeply at ease, serene	Body fully relaxed, slow breathing

✎ My Personal Emotional Warning Signs

I know I am at a 7 or above when I feel: ______________________ Physical signs that I'm escalating:

______________________ The emotional state most likely to lead me to gamble: ______________________

My usual level when the day starts: __________ My level when I am most vulnerable to gambling

urges: ____

6.3 Emotional Regulation Techniques

1. The STOP Technique

Stop what you are doing. **T**ake a breath. **O**bserve what is happening inside — thoughts, feelings, body sensations. **P**roceed with awareness and intention. The STOP technique interrupts automatic responses before they become behaviors.

2. Deep Breathing (4-7-8 Method)

Inhale through the nose for **4 counts**. Hold the breath for **7 counts**. Exhale completely through the mouth for **8 counts**. Repeat 3–4 times. This technique activates the parasympathetic nervous system, reducing physiological arousal and creating space between urge and action.

3. Grounding (5-4-3-2-1 Senses)

Name **5 things you can see, 4 things you can physically feel, 3 things you can hear, 2 things you can smell, 1 thing you can taste**. This exercise anchors attention to the present moment, reducing the intensity of gambling-related thoughts and urges.

4. Progressive Muscle Relaxation

Systematically tense and release major muscle groups from feet to face, holding each contraction for 5–10 seconds before releasing. This technique reduces the physical tension that often accompanies emotional distress and gambling urges.

5. Urge Surfing

Instead of fighting or giving in to an urge, observe it with curiosity. Notice where you feel it in your body. Notice its intensity rising — and then, inevitably, falling. Like a wave, urges peak and pass. Urge surfing builds confidence that urges are survivable without acting on them.

6. Opposite Action

From Dialectical Behavior Therapy (DBT): when an emotion is pushing you toward a harmful action (gambling), deliberately do the opposite. If anxiety makes you want to escape through gambling, instead reach out to a support person. If shame makes you want to hide, instead be honest with someone you trust.

7. Mindfulness Check-In

Pause and ask yourself: "What am I feeling right now? Where do I feel it in my body? What does this emotion need from me?" Simply naming an emotion reduces its intensity — a process neurobiologists call "affect labeling."

8. Physical Discharge

Physical exercise — walking, running, swimming, or any movement — is one of the most effective interventions for emotional dysregulation and gambling urges. Even a 10-minute brisk walk can significantly reduce urge intensity.

6.4 My Emotional Management Plan Worksheet

✎ **Worksheet 6.4 — My Emotional Management Plan**

My top 3 emotional triggers for gambling:

1. ______________________ 2. ______________________ 3. ______________________

My early warning signs (emotional, physical, behavioral): My coping skills at MILD distress (levels

1–4): My coping skills at MODERATE distress (levels 5–7): My coping skills at SEVERE distress

(levels 8–10): My personal crisis plan (who to call, where to go, what to

say):____

Module 7: Family and Recovery

Family Impact · Letter to My Family · Rebuilding Trust · Genogram · Involving Family

7.1 Impact of Gambling on the Family

Gambling disorder is rarely an individual's problem alone — it is, in most cases, a family disorder. The entire family system is affected by one member's gambling, often in ways that are profound, long-lasting, and clinically significant in their own right.

Financial Stress: Gambling disorder depletes family resources in ways that can be devastating — depleted savings, missed mortgage payments, secret loans, and debt incurred in family members' names without their knowledge. Research suggests that the average gambling disorder patient carries gambling-related debts of $40,000 or more by the time they enter treatment.

Broken Trust: The deception that accompanies gambling disorder — the lies about whereabouts, finances, and behavior — erodes the foundational trust of family relationships. Trust, once broken, is rebuilt slowly and requires sustained honest effort over time.

Emotional Unavailability: The person with gambling disorder is often preoccupied — planning the next gambling episode, recovering from the last one, or managing the anxiety of concealment. This preoccupation means emotional absence from family, even when physically present.

Co-dependency and Enabling: Family members often develop patterns — covering debts, making excuses, providing money to "help" — that inadvertently enable the continuation of gambling. These patterns develop from love and fear, not weakness, but they require clinical attention.

Children: Children in families affected by gambling disorder are at elevated risk for anxiety, depression, academic difficulties, and the development of their own gambling or substance use problems. Research indicates that children who grow up in homes with a gambling-disordered parent are 2–4 times more likely to develop problem gambling themselves.

7.2 Letter to My Family Worksheet

✎ Worksheet 7.2 — Letter to My Family

Choose one significant family member or loved one who has been affected by your gambling. This letter is a private writing exercise — you do not need to share it unless and until you choose to do so with the support of your counselor.

I am writing this letter to: ______________________

What I want you to know about my gambling:

What I am sorry for:

What I am doing to change:

What I need from you in my recovery:

What I hope for our relationship:

7.3 Rebuilding Trust

Trust is rebuilt through consistent action over time — not through promises, apologies, or explanations alone. The stages of trust rebuilding in the context of gambling recovery follow a predictable pattern:

1. **Acknowledgment:** Openly acknowledging what happened — the gambling, the deception, the harm — without minimizing or explaining it away. This is the foundation. Without it, the process cannot begin.
2. **Accountability:** Taking full responsibility for your actions and their impact. Not blaming circumstances, others, or the addiction itself. Accountability means owning the choices you made and their consequences.
3. **Consistent Action:** Making and keeping promises, small and large, over an extended period. Every kept commitment is a building block. Every broken promise sets the process back significantly.
4. **Time:** Trust is rebuilt on a timeline determined by the person who was hurt, not by the person who

caused the harm. Recovery requires accepting this and continuing consistent action even when recognition is slow in coming.

✎ **My Trust-Rebuilding Plan**

Person I am working to rebuild trust with: ______________________ Specific actions I will take to

demonstrate trustworthiness: Commitments I will make and keep: How I will handle setbacks

without giving up on the process:

7.4 Family Addiction Genogram

A family addiction genogram is a visual map of addiction-related patterns across multiple generations of your family. Research on gambling disorder consistently shows strong familial transmission — both genetic and environmental. Creating a genogram helps you understand the broader context of your gambling disorder, identify family patterns, and recognize the impact your recovery can have on future generations.

How to Create Your Genogram:

1. Use squares (□) to represent males and circles (○) to represent females.
2. Connect partners with a horizontal line and children with vertical lines below.
3. Mark individuals with known gambling problems with a "G" inside the shape.
4. Mark individuals with substance use issues with an "S."
5. Mark individuals with other compulsive behaviors (compulsive shopping, etc.) with a "C."
6. Include at least three generations: grandparents, parents/aunts/uncles, and your generation.

My Family Genogram (draw below)

Grandparents' Generation:

Parents' Generation:

My Generation:

Legend: □ = Male ○ = Female G = Gambling Issue S = Substance Use C = Other Compulsive Behavior // = Divorced

What patterns do you notice in your family genogram?

7.5 Involving Family in Recovery

Involving family in your recovery — when appropriate and when both parties are willing — can significantly strengthen your recovery outcomes. It also provides family members with the support and information they need to heal from the impact of your gambling.

Practical Steps for Family Involvement:

- Invite a trusted family member to a counseling session when you and your counselor agree the time is right.
- Encourage affected family members to attend Gam-Anon meetings (a 12-step program for families of gamblers).
- Consider structured family therapy with a clinician experienced in addiction and family systems.
- Be transparent about your recovery activities — meetings attended, counseling sessions, milestones celebrated.
- Set clear, mutual expectations for communication about finances, accountability, and recovery.

✎ Family Involvement Readiness Checklist

☐ I have discussed involving family with my counselor.

☐ I have identified which family members are safe and supportive to involve.

☐ I am prepared to be honest — not defensive — in family conversations.

☐ I have information about Gam-Anon to share with affected family members.

☐ I am willing to accept family members' reactions without withdrawing from recovery.

☐ I understand that family healing takes time, just as my recovery does.

Module 8: Problem Solving and Coping Skills

Problem-Solving Model · Solving My Problems · Healthy Alternatives · Weekly Activity Plan · Assertive Communication

8.1 The Problem-Solving Model

Many individuals turn to gambling as a misguided attempt to solve problems — financial pressure, relationship stress, career difficulties. Learning effective problem-solving skills is therefore a core recovery competency. The 5-step problem-solving model provides a structured, evidence-based approach to addressing life's challenges without turning to gambling.

Step	Action	Description
1	Define the Problem	State the problem clearly and specifically. "I have too much debt" is vague. "I owe $3,200 on a credit card at 24% interest and cannot make the minimum payment" is actionable.
2	Generate Options	Brainstorm as many solutions as possible without evaluating them. Include options that seem impractical. Quantity over quality at this stage.
3	Evaluate Options	Review each option for feasibility, pros, cons, and potential consequences. Eliminate options that are harmful or unrealistic.
4	Choose and Act	Select the best option and take the first concrete step. Identify a specific action you can take within 24 hours.
5	Evaluate Results	After implementing the solution, assess the outcome. Did it work? What needs adjustment? Problem-solving is iterative.

Worked Example

Problem: "I'm stressed about a large overdue bill and I feel the urge to gamble to try to win the money to pay it."

Options generated: (a) Call the creditor and request a payment plan, (b) Gamble to try to win the money, (c) Ask a family member for a small loan, (d) Look into credit counseling, (e) Prioritize this bill by cutting other expenses temporarily.

Eliminated: Option (b) — gambling would most likely increase the debt, not solve it.

Chosen: Options (a) and (d) — call creditor today and research NFCC credit counseling.

Result: Creditor agreed to a payment plan. Stress reduced significantly. Gambling urge passed.

8.2 Solving My Problems Worksheet

✎ Worksheet 8.2 — Applying the 5-Step Model to My Problem

Step 1 — Define the Problem Clearly and Specifically: Step 2 — Generate Options (brainstorm

freely, no filtering):

a.____

b.____

c.____

d.____

e.____

____

Step 3 — Evaluate Each Option (pros, cons, feasibility): Step 4 — My Chosen Solution and First

Action Step (within 24 hours): Step 5 — Outcome (complete after acting):

8.3 Healthy Alternatives to Gambling

The following alternatives are organized by the underlying need that gambling may have been meeting. Finding activities that genuinely meet those needs — in healthy ways — is a cornerstone of lifestyle recovery.

Need Gambling Was Meeting	Healthy Alternatives
Boredom / Excitement-Seeking	Physical exercise (running, martial arts, cycling), competitive sports or games, live music or sports events, travel, cooking new cuisines, rock climbing or outdoor adventure
Anxiety / Stress Relief	Meditation or mindfulness practice, yoga, deep breathing exercises, journaling, therapy, nature walks, hot bath or shower, soothing music

Social Connection	Gamblers Anonymous meetings, faith community involvement, volunteering, community classes, reconnecting with old friends, joining a club or team, family dinners
Financial Hope / Escape from Debt	Meeting with a credit counselor (NFCC), setting a structured debt repayment plan, reading personal finance books, taking a free financial literacy course, selling unused items
Escape from Problems	Therapy or counseling, journaling about the problem, calling a trusted friend, watching a film or reading, a brief walk to change your mental state, problem-solving (Module 8.1)

8.4 Weekly Activity Plan Worksheet

Use this grid to plan healthy, meaningful activities for the week ahead. Scheduling activities in advance fills the time that gambling previously occupied and creates a structured recovery environment.

Day	Morning	Afternoon	Evening
Monday			
Tuesday			
Wednesday			
Thursday			
Friday			
Saturday			

Sunday

8.5 Assertive Communication Skills

Recovery frequently requires navigating social situations that involve gambling — invitations to casinos, requests for money, family confrontations. Developing assertive communication skills empowers you to navigate these situations without resorting to aggression or passivity.

Style	Characteristics	Recovery Risk
Passive	Avoiding conflict, agreeing when you don't want to, not expressing needs	May agree to gamble to avoid conflict; doesn't ask for help when needed
Aggressive	Demanding, blaming, threatening, dismissing others' feelings	Creates conflict that becomes a gambling trigger; damages support relationships
Assertive	Clear, honest, respectful; expressing needs and limits while honoring others' dignity	Lowest risk; builds support and creates authentic communication

Assertive Communication Scripts for Recovery Situations:

1. **Declining a casino invitation:** "Thanks for thinking of me — I'm not doing that anymore. I'd love to hang out though — could we do dinner or catch a game instead?"
2. **Asking for help:** "I want to be honest with you. I'm struggling right now and I could really use your support. Can we talk?"
3. **Setting a boundary with an enabling family member:** "I know you want to help, and I love you for it. But lending me money right now isn't helping me recover. What would really help is if you came to a counseling session with me."
4. **Responding to pressure to gamble:** "I appreciate the offer, but gambling is something I've had to

give up completely. It's not negotiable for me, and I hope you can respect that."

5. **Telling a new employer or school about your situation (if appropriate):** "I'm in recovery from a behavioral health condition. I'm fully functional and committed, and I wanted to be transparent with you as I build a new chapter."

✎ Assertive Communication Practice

A situation where I need to communicate more assertively in my recovery:

____

How I have handled it in the past (passive, aggressive, or assertive?):

____

My assertive script for this situation:__________________________________

____

Module 9: Financial Recovery

Assessing Financial Damage · Creating a Recovery Budget · Financial Protection · My Financial Recovery Plan

9.1 Assessing Financial Damage

One of the most painful aspects of gambling disorder is confronting the financial consequences. Many individuals in early recovery avoid this assessment out of shame or fear — but an honest financial picture is essential to building a recovery plan that is grounded in reality. You cannot navigate out of a crisis without knowing where you are starting from.

✎ Financial Damage Assessment

Total estimated gambling losses to date (to the best of your knowledge): $___________ Current

Outstanding Debts:

Creditor / Lender	Amount Owed	Interest Rate	Monthly Minimum
	$	%	$
	$	%	$
	$	%	$
	$	%	$
	$	%	$
TOTAL	$	—	$

Monthly Income: $__________ Monthly Essential Expenses (rent, food, utilities, transportation): $__________ Monthly Debt Payments: $__________ Net Monthly Position (income minus expenses and debt payments): $__________ Assets (savings, property, retirement accounts, other): __________

9.2 Creating a Recovery Budget

A structured budget is not a punishment — it is a tool for freedom. In recovery from gambling disorder, a budget provides clarity, reduces financial anxiety, and removes the ambiguity about money that can trigger relapse. Complete this monthly budget template honestly and review it with your counselor or a financial advisor.

INCOME	
Wages / Salary (take-home)	$__________
Other Income (benefits, support, etc.)	$__________
Total Monthly Income	**$__________**
ESSENTIAL EXPENSES	
Rent / Mortgage	$__________
Utilities (electric, gas, water)	$__________
Food / Groceries	$__________
Transportation (car payment, gas, transit)	$__________
Medical / Prescriptions	$__________
Phone	$__________
Child Care / Other Essentials	$__________
Total Essential Expenses	**$__________**
DEBT REPAYMENT	
Priority Debt #1	$__________
Priority Debt #2	$__________
Other Debt Payments	$__________
Total Debt Repayment	**$__________**
SAVINGS AND DISCRETIONARY	
Emergency Savings	$__________
Discretionary (personal spending, recreation)	$__________

TOTAL MONTHLY BUDGET **$__________**

Surplus / Deficit **$__________**

Gambling-Proofing Your Budget

- Remove all discretionary cash from your access. Carry only the amount needed for planned purchases.
- Use direct deposit and automatic bill pay so essential bills are paid before you can access the money.
- Avoid ATMs near casinos, gambling venues, or online betting sites.
- Consider temporarily giving financial management to a trusted family member or financial advisor.

9.3 Financial Protection Strategies

Complete the following checklist of financial protection strategies. Check off steps you have already taken and circle steps you will take within the next 30 days.

Done	Plan to Do	Financial Protection Strategy
☐	○	Enrolled in casino/venue self-exclusion program(s)
☐	○	Removed or blocked gambling apps from phone and devices
☐	○	Installed gambling-blocking software (GamBlock, BetFilter, etc.)
☐	○	Removed ATM cards / limited access to cash
☐	○	Temporarily transferred financial management to a trusted person
☐	○	Set up automatic bill pay for all essential expenses
☐	○	Requested a credit freeze to prevent new credit accounts
☐	○	Closed or suspended online gambling accounts

- ☐ ○ Removed credit cards from online gambling site accounts
- ☐ ○ Contacted a nonprofit credit counseling agency (NFCC)
- ☐ ○ Discussed finances openly and honestly with family
- ☐ ○ Created and am following a written recovery budget

9.4 My Financial Recovery Plan Worksheet

✎ Worksheet 9.4 — My Financial Recovery Plan

Short-Term Financial Goals (within 30 days): Short-Term Financial Goals (within 60–90

days):____

____

Long-Term Financial Goals (1 year): Long-Term Financial Goals (5 years):__________

____

Debt Repayment Priority List (highest interest first):

1. ______________________ $________

2. ______________________ $________

3. ______________________ $________

Financial Support Resources I Will Use:

☐ NFCC Credit Counseling: 1-800-388-2227 / www.nfcc.org

☐ NCPG Financial Assistance Hotline: 1-800-522-4700

☐ Local bankruptcy attorney (consultation only)

☐ Financial advisor / planner: Name: ____________________

Module 10: Relapse Prevention

Understanding Relapse · Early Warning Signs · My Emergency Plan · High-Risk Analysis · If I Have a Slip

10.1 Understanding Relapse

Relapse is best understood as a *process*, not an event. The gambling behavior that constitutes a relapse is typically the final visible step in a chain of warning signs, decisions, and emotional drift that began days, weeks, or even months earlier. Understanding this is not permission to relapse — it is the essential knowledge needed to prevent relapse by intervening early in the process.

Clinically, it is useful to distinguish between two terms:

- **Lapse:** A single, isolated gambling incident after a period of abstinence. A lapse is serious and requires immediate clinical attention — but it is not the end of recovery. How you respond to a lapse determines whether it remains a lapse or becomes a full relapse.
- **Relapse:** A return to the full previous pattern of gambling behavior — in frequency, duration, and amounts. Relapse represents a breakdown of the recovery plan and requires a comprehensive clinical reassessment and renewed commitment to treatment.

The Marlatt Relapse Prevention Model (1985) identifies key factors that contribute to relapse: high-risk situations, coping skill deficits, outcome expectancies (believing gambling will produce positive results), and the Abstinence Violation Effect (the destructive self-talk that follows a lapse: "I've already failed — I might as well keep going"). Recovery requires addressing each of these factors proactively.

An Important Truth About Relapse

A slip does not erase your recovery. Every day of recovery is real and permanent. A setback is information, not a verdict. The most important thing you can do after a slip is not to gamble again — but to reach out for support immediately and return to treatment without delay. Shame and isolation after a slip are the most dangerous responses. Connection and honesty are the most healing ones.

10.2 Early Warning Signs

Review the following early warning signs of impending relapse. Check any that you recognize in yourself — past or present.

Emotional / Psychological Warning Signs

☐ Warning Sign
☐ Restlessness, irritability, or unexplained agitation
☐ Romanticizing gambling — remembering wins, minimizing losses
☐ Overconfidence about recovery ("I've got this — I don't need meetings anymore")
☐ Increasing depression, hopelessness, or emptiness

☐ Social withdrawal and increasing isolation

☐ Feeling that recovery isn't worth it or that life is boring without gambling

Behavioral Warning Signs

☐ Warning Sign
☐ Skipping or stopping counseling sessions or GA meetings
☐ Avoiding accountability partner or sponsor
☐ Lying about small things — a return to the habit of deception
☐ Financial secrecy — hiding spending or not reviewing the budget
☐ Driving past or near casinos, checking gambling apps "out of curiosity"
☐ Dropping recovery rituals (journaling, exercise, daily check-ins)

Cognitive Warning Signs

☐ Warning Sign
☐ Gambling thoughts returning frequently and feeling difficult to dismiss
☐ Minimizing past consequences: "It wasn't that bad"
☐ Bargaining thoughts: "Just once, on a special occasion, wouldn't hurt"
☐ Entertaining fantasy plans about controlled gambling

✎ My Personal Warning Sign Checklist

The warning signs most specific to ME — the ones I know from experience:__________

____

When I notice these signs, I will:____

____

10.3 My Emergency Plan

MY GAMBLING EMERGENCY RESPONSE PLAN

My personal warning signs are: When I feel the urge to gamble, I will immediately: My first

call will be to:

Name: ______________________ Phone: ______________________

My second call will be to:

Name: ______________________ Phone: ______________________

If I am near a gambling venue, I will remove myself by:____________________________

Phrases I will say to myself when an urge hits: My safe place (where I will go if I feel I might

gamble):____

National Problem Gambling Helpline (24/7): 1-800-522-4700

10.4 High-Risk Situation Analysis Worksheet

Use this table to analyze high-risk situations as they occur. Recording and reviewing these situations with your counselor builds your relapse prevention skills over time.

Date	Situation Description	Thoughts and Feelings	Urge Intensity (1–10)	Coping Strategies Used	Outcome

10.5 If I Have a Slip...

If you have a gambling slip, the most important thing is how you respond. Below is a compassionate, evidence-based response protocol. Read this section now, when you are calm — and refer back to it if a slip occurs.

1. **Stop immediately.** Leave the gambling environment as soon as you are aware of what is happening. Do not try to "win back" what you spent during the slip — this is chasing and will worsen the outcome.
2. **Contact your counselor or sponsor within 24 hours.** This is the most important action you can take. Do not wait until your next scheduled appointment. Call today.
3. **Do not isolate.** Isolation after a slip is one of the most dangerous patterns. Reach out to someone in your support network — even if you feel ashamed. Especially if you feel ashamed.
4. **Identify what triggered the slip.** As soon as you are safe and calm, review the chain of events that led to the slip. What was the trigger? What thoughts preceded the gambling? Where did the relapse process begin?
5. **Return to treatment without shame.** A slip is not a moral failure — it is clinical information. It tells

you where your relapse prevention plan needs strengthening. Use it constructively.

6. **Review and strengthen your relapse prevention plan.** Work with your counselor to identify what was missing from your plan and add new strategies. The goal is a stronger plan going forward, not punishment for the past.

✎ Post-Slip Reflection Worksheet

What happened leading up to the slip (describe the chain of events):________________

____

What was I feeling before the slip?____

What thoughts preceded the gambling?____

Where was the earliest point where I could have intervened?______________________

What will I do differently next time?____

A compassionate message I want to give myself right now:_________________________

Module 11: Building a New Life

Recovery Vision · SMART Goals · Support Network · Community Resources · Commitment · Daily Affirmations

11.1 My Recovery Vision

Recovery is not simply about stopping gambling — it is about building a life that is meaningful, connected, and fulfilling enough that gambling no longer holds appeal. This begins with a vision. Take a moment to settle yourself, breathe deeply, and allow yourself to imagine your life one year from now, fully in recovery.

✎ My Recovery Vision (One Year From Now)

Imagine your life one year into solid recovery. What does it look like? Be as vivid and specific as possible. This is your vision — allow it to be hopeful and ambitious.

How do I feel each morning when I wake up?______________________________________

What do my relationships look like?____

Who is in my life?____

What is my financial situation?____

What have I accomplished that I'm proud of?______________________________

What does a typical, healthy day in my recovered life look like?________________

____

What word or phrase best describes the person I am becoming? _______________

____

11.2 Setting SMART Goals

SMART goals are goals that are **S**pecific, **M**easurable, **A**chievable, **R**elevant, and **T**ime-bound. Setting SMART goals in recovery gives your vision a concrete structure and creates clear milestones of progress.

Component	Question to Ask	Example
Specific	Exactly what will I do?	"I will attend Gamblers Anonymous meetings."

Measurable	How will I know I've achieved it?	"I will attend 3 meetings per week."
Achievable	Is this realistic given my current situation?	"There are 5 GA meetings per week in my area."
Relevant	Does this support my recovery vision?	"GA meetings provide community and accountability."
Time-bound	By when will I achieve this?	"I will maintain this for the next 90 days."

✎ My SMART Recovery Goals

Short-Term Goal (within 30 days):

My goal: ____

How I'll measure success: ____________________ **Target date:** ____________________

Medium-Term Goal (within 3–6 months):

My goal: ____

How I'll measure success: ____________________ **Target date:** ____________________

Long-Term Goal (1 year):

My goal: ____

How I'll measure success: ____________________ **Target date:** ____________________

11.3 Support Network

No one recovers alone. Building a strong, diverse support network is one of the most powerful protective factors against relapse. The concentric circle model below helps you map your network across three levels of closeness and intensity of support.

◆ **Inner Circle — Closest Supporters (daily/weekly contact, know your full story)**

Names and contact info: ____

____

◆ Middle Circle — Regular Supporters (counselor, sponsor, GA friends, trusted

colleagues)

Names and contact info:____

____

◆ Outer Circle — Community Resources (GA group, faith community, helplines,

professional services)

Names and contact info:____

____

GA / Recovery Meeting Tracker:

Date	Meeting Name / Location	Notes / How I Felt

11.4 Community Resources

Gamblers Anonymous (GA)

Website: www.gamblersanonymous.org | Helpline: 1-800-522-4700

A 12-step fellowship for individuals with gambling problems. Meetings available nationwide and internationally, in-person and online.

National Council on Problem Gambling Helpline

1-800-522-4700 (available 24 hours a day, 7 days a week)

Provides crisis support, referrals to treatment, and information about problem gambling resources nationwide.

Gam-Anon (for families and loved ones of gamblers)

Website: www.gam-anon.org

A support group for the family members, friends, and loved ones of those affected by gambling disorder.

SAMHSA National Helpline

1-800-662-4357 (free, confidential, 24/7)

Treatment referral and information service for mental health and substance use disorders. Also accessible via text: text "HELLO" to 435748.

National Foundation for Credit Counseling (NFCC)

Website: www.nfcc.org | Phone: 1-800-388-2227

Nonprofit credit and debt counseling services to help rebuild financial stability in recovery.

Crisis Text Line

Text HOME to 741741

Free, 24/7 text-based crisis support for anyone in a difficult moment, including gambling-related crises.

Gambling Therapy App

Available free at www.gamblingtherapy.org — online support, forums, and professional guidance for problem gamblers worldwide.

My Local Resources:

Local GA Meeting (time/location): ______________________________________

My Counselor: ______________________________ **Phone:** __________________

My Sponsor: ________________________________ **Phone:** __________________

Other Local Resource: ____

11.5 My Commitment to Recovery

MY COMMITMENT TO RECOVERY

I, ______________________________, on this date __________, make this commitment to my

recovery and to the life I am choosing to build. I acknowledge that gambling has caused

harm to myself and to those I love. I accept responsibility for my choices and my recovery.

I understand that recovery requires ongoing effort, honesty, and connection — and I

commit to bringing all of these to my journey. My personal statement of commitment (in my

own words): The most important thing I am recovering FOR:____________________________

Signature: _________________________ Date: __________

Witness Signature (optional): ________________ **Date:** _______

11.6 Daily Affirmations

Affirmations are brief, positive statements that, practiced consistently, help rewire thought patterns and reinforce a recovery identity. Read these aloud each morning, or choose the ones that resonate most with you and write them where you will see them daily.

1. *I am stronger than my urges, and I grow stronger every day I choose recovery.*

2. *Every day of recovery is a gift I give to myself and to the people I love.*

3. *I am rebuilding trust — with myself and with others — one honest day at a time.*

4. *My past does not define my future. I am more than my addiction.*

5. *I choose financial freedom and peace of mind over temporary relief.*

6. *I am worthy of a full, meaningful, and connected life without gambling.*

7. *I have survived the darkest moments — and I carry that strength with me today.*

8. *Recovery is not a destination — it is a practice, and I show up for it daily.*

9. *I am not alone. I am surrounded by people who want me to succeed.*

10. *I can feel difficult emotions without acting on them. I trust my ability to cope.*

11. *Every honest word I speak is an act of recovery.*

12. *I am reclaiming my time, my money, and my relationships.*

13. *I am allowed to take up space in my own recovery. My needs matter.*

14. I choose to face my problems with clarity and courage rather than escape.

15. The urge to gamble is temporary. My commitment to recovery is permanent.

16. I am grateful for one more day to choose differently.

17. I am learning to find joy in simple, real, lasting things.

18. My recovery is not only for me — it is a gift to everyone who loves me.

19. I deserve peace, stability, and the life I am building.

20. I am enough, right now, exactly as I am — and I am getting better every day.

Appendix A: Daily Recovery Log

Photocopy this page for daily use

DAILY RECOVERY LOG

Date: **Day of Recovery:** **Overall Mood (1–10):**

Gambling urge today? ☐ Yes ☐ No	**Urge intensity (1–10):**

Trigger identified (what brought on any urge today?): Coping skill I used today: Support contact

made today? ☐ Yes ☐ No Who: ____________________ Today I am grateful for: One thing I did

well today: Tomorrow I will:

"You don't have to see the whole staircase — just take the next step." — Martin Luther King Jr.

Appendix B: Gambling Urge Tracking Log

Weekly urge tracking table — photocopy as needed

Use this log to track gambling urges throughout the week. Recording urges — even when you did not gamble — builds self-awareness and provides valuable information for your counselor. Urges recorded and reviewed are urges understood.

Date / Time	Situation (Where / What Was Happening)	Urge Intensity (1-10)	Thoughts / Self-Talk	Action Taken	Outcome

Weekly Reflection

At the end of each week, review your urge log and ask: What patterns do I notice? Which situations were highest risk? Which coping strategies worked best? Bring this log to your next counseling session or GA meeting.

Appendix C: Recommended Resources and Hotlines

Keep this page accessible — in your wallet, on your phone, or on your refrigerator

Crisis and Helpline Resources

Resource	Contact	Available
National Problem Gambling Helpline Crisis counseling, referrals, information	1-800-522-4700	24/7
Crisis Text Line Text-based crisis support	Text HOME to 741741	24/7
SAMHSA National Helpline Mental health and substance use treatment referrals	1-800-662-4357	24/7
National Suicide Prevention Lifeline Crisis support	988 (call or text)	24/7

Support Organizations

Organization	Website	Description
Gamblers Anonymous	www.gamblersanonymous.org	12-step fellowship for problem gamblers; meeting finder, online meetings
Gam-Anon	www.gam-anon.org	Support for families and loved ones of

		gamblers
National Council on Problem Gambling	www.ncpgambling.org	Advocacy, resources, treatment finder, research
Gambling Therapy	www.gamblingtherapy.org	Free online support, forums, and professional guidance
GamCare	www.gamcare.org.uk	International resources, online counseling, self-help tools

Financial Resources

Resource	Contact	Description
National Foundation for Credit Counseling (NFCC)	1-800-388-2227 / www.nfcc.org	Nonprofit credit counseling, debt management plans
Consumer Financial Protection Bureau	www.consumerfinance.gov	Free financial tools and education

Apps and Digital Tools

App / Tool	Platform	Description
Gambling Therapy App	iOS / Android / Web	Online support, self-exclusion tools, progress tracking
GamStop	www.gamstop.co.uk	UK-based national self-exclusion scheme for online gambling
BetBlocker	iOS / Android / Desktop	Free gambling-blocking software for multiple devices
Headspace / Calm	iOS / Android	Mindfulness and meditation apps supportive of

emotional regulation

Recommended Reading

- *Behind the 8-Ball: A Recovery Guide for the Families of Gamblers* — Linda Berman & Mary-Ellen Siegel
- *Overcoming Your Pathological Gambling: Workbook* — Robert Ladouceur & Stella Lachance
- *The Urge: Our History of Addiction* — Carl Erik Fisher, MD
- *Recovery: Freedom from Our Addictions* — Russell Brand
- *Quit Gambling: A Practical Guide* — Joanna Franklin

My Key Contacts (fill in and carry with you):

My Counselor: ______________________ Phone: ______________________

My Sponsor / Support: ______________________ Phone: ______________________

GA Meeting Day/Time: ______________________ Location: ______________________

Crisis Line: **1-800-522-4700**

Appendix D: Notes

Use these pages for reflections, session notes, or personal writing

Notes:

Notes:

Notes:

"Your journey toward healing begins here."

www.ingramcontent.com/pod-product-compliance
Lightning Source LLC
LaVergne TN
LVHW082354200926
848481LV00012B/3565
* 9 7 9 8 9 9 6 1 0 0 9 1 0 *